PURSUIT OF TITUS

Unveiling True Sonship

Prophet Shepherd Bushiri

Cover designed by Reach Publishers
Website: www.reachpublishers.co.za
E-mail - reach@webstorm.co.za

All Scriptures are quoted from either the King James Version or New International Version, unless otherwise indicated.

For further information, permission, orders or comments, contact:
Shepherd Bushiri Ministries at:
ministryprophetic@gmail.com
www.psbministries.org

Contents

INTRODUCTION

In this book, *The Pursuit of Titus*, I present one of the sons of Apostle Paul, called Titus. I have given this book this title in order to encourage and provoke you to pursue the kind of devotion and submission that Titus had. Paul and Titus shared a special bond, so much so that Paul trusted him and singled him out as a "true son". This book is a testimony to the genuine sonship of Titus. It is for this reason that the subtitle of this book is, *Unveiling True Sonship*.

True sonship is a mystery that must be unveiled. It is my conviction that as you read this book, you will be encouraged to pursue the manner of sonship which Paul referred to as, true sonship.

God in His infinite wisdom decided that He would rule the earth through those who are like Him, His sons and daughters. Because of His great love, He made himself vulnerable to His beloved children when He gave them dominion over the earth (Gen 1:26). Since that time all that He wished to do in the earth realm, He does through man. It is for such reasons, that when He wanted to deliver man, He sent His son as a man.

Understand this; God does nothing in the earth realm without a man. Look at this Scripture in the book of Ezekiel:

> *"**I looked for someone among them** who would build up the wall and stand before me **in the gap on behalf of the land** so I would not have to destroy it, but **I found no one. So I will pour out my wrath on them** and consume them with my fiery anger, bringing down on their own heads all they have done, declares the Sovereign* LORD."
>
> ~Ez 22:31-32~

Look at that, the will of God was to have mercy on the people but because He could not find a man to partner with in the execution of His plan, He had no choice, but to send judgment. Now if God does nothing without a man why is it that believers think that for success in life all they need is God? I don't care how dire your situation is, but know this, God will never come down from heaven to deliver you from it, if He never came down when His beloved son Jesus cried out to Him from the cross, what makes you think He will come down to you because you are experiencing a challenge? God still looks for a man. He pours himself out onto a man and partners with him to do His will. If you want God, find a man who is carrying God and then submit under that man.

This book is about submitting to a man who carries God, a man who fathers you in the spirit. It is this man that I will be referring to as a spiritual father. The centurion understood this very well (Mt 8:9). He knew that to exercise power you need to be under power, it is a spiritual principle. If you want to walk in greater dimensions of God's power and glory, you need to submit to someone who already walks in what you desire and then the anointing will flow from him down to you. Thus, the anointing always flows from the head down. The time has come for the church to stop being divided, but to start gathering around fathers, to follow men and women of God who follow God. I have tried it and it works!! Submission has done more for my ministry and personal walk with God than all the prayer and fasting in the world could have ever achieved.

1

SONSHIP AND FATHERHOOD

The concept of "sonship" or "spiritual sonship" is often met with reservation, particularly by some women who view it as a discriminatory term that excludes females. It is important that we are clear on this, that the word has nothing to do with gender; instead, it refers to a posture of submission and maturity and is therefore, equally applicable to both males and females. It is used to distinguish those who have grown spiritually from those who are still babies in the Lord. Understand that there is a significant difference between children and sons, they approach the things of God differently. Paul being a spiritual father to Titus provided the following description of sons:

For as many as are ***led by the Spirit of God, they are the sons of God****.*

~Rom 8:14~

I would like to draw your attention to two truths embedded in this Scripture. Firstly, there is an inclusion criteria to becoming a son of God and it is simply yielding to the leadership of the Spirit of God. So if one is led by the Spirit, they qualify for sonship. The second truth is closely related to the first, sonship is in essence about submitting to leadership. For the Spirit to lead you, He must be your leader and you must be the follower. Ability to follow is a sure sign of maturity. Only the mature are able to yield to leadership. In fact, maturity empowers one to submit. Sons are mature, they have grown to a level where they are not tossed to and fro, neither are they easily mislead by the things of the world, instead, the Holy Spirit is their guider and teacher (Jn 14:26, 16:13). This does not mean that since a son is led by the Holy Spirit, he does not need a spiritual father; instead, because of the leading by the Holy Spirit, the need for a spiritual father becomes even greater. It is not only those who are young in the Lord who need a spiritual father, instead everyone who claims to be a son of God because God established parenthood as a way of passing on inheritance. Thus, since God is Spirit, a son needs those who are spiritually mature, to guide him in spiritual matters.

Follow my example, as I follow the example of Christ.

~1Cor 11:1~

Christ is available to all, and we can learn about His life from the Bible, yet, Paul instructed the church in Corinth to follow him as he followed Christ. We see Paul including himself as a middleman of sorts. I know that I will lose a lot of religious folks here, but I need you to follow me very closely so that you can be liberated from the spirit of religion. In this verse, Paul was addressing his spiritual children, whom he was grooming to become sons. He was nurturing them to grow from being children in the things of God, so that they mature into sons. Parents play the most crucial role in the development of their children. To a large extent, who you are today is a sum total of the example or lack of an example set by your parents. Psychologists have discovered that parents are ordained models of life in the natural[1]. The same is also true in the spiritual realm. Paul by the election of God, was a spiritual father to them in order to be a living model of the life of Christ. All that Christ is, He learnt it from His Father in heaven. Do you see that? Paul was

---

[1] Taber, J. B., Hartung, J. P., Briddick, H., Briddick, C. W., & Rehfuss, C. M. (2011). Career style interview: A contextualized approach to career counselling. *The Career Development Quarterly*, 59. 274- 287.

following the pattern already set by God through His Beloved Son Jesus Christ. God is Spirit, and it is not an easy process for a natural man, who has just been converted to tune into the things of the Spirit. As such, a spiritual father helps to bridge this gap, by serving as an example or a model of God the Father. It is through this relationship that a person is mentored and guided to become all that God has created him to be. Many people might not like it or even agree with it but it is the way of God and that makes it perfect! That is why Paul had the boldness to invite his sons to follow his example. As a spiritual father myself, and also a spiritual son to my spiritual father, Senior Major Prophet Uebert Angel, I am fully convinced that no one can claim to be a son of God unless that person also submits under an earthly spiritual father. The Bible states that:

> *... For whoever* ***does not love their brother and sister, whom they have seen, cannot love God, whom they have not seen.***
>
> ~1Jn 4:20~

The principle that underlies the above verse is crystal clear: if you cannot love the person who is seen (natural), you cannot claim to love God whom you cannot see (spiritual). Similarly, if you cannot submit to a spiritual father whom you can see, you cannot claim to be submissive to God whom you cannot see! Paul knew that Christ was accessible to all his spiritual children through the Word of God, or revelation like he had access to him. However, he still maintained that they must follow him as he followed Christ and this would assist them to be better followers of Christ.

Apostle Paul probably had one of the most peculiar and dramatic conversion experiences recorded in the Bible. He was a man who was vehemently opposed to the gospel of Jesus Christ but a solitary revelatory encounter with Jesus transformed his life eternally. From that day henceforth, his life was marked by revelation. In one of his letters, he states the following:

> *I want you to know, brothers and sisters, that* ***the gospel I preached is not of human origin.*** *I did not receive it from any man, nor was I taught it; rather,* ***I received it by revelation from Jesus Christ.***
>
> ~Gal 1:11~

Notice from the above verse that, although Paul never met Jesus physically, he had a spiritual encounter with Him wherein Jesus revealed the mysteries of the gospel to him (Acts 9). One of the things that led to the gospel that Paul preached to stand out is that, God did not use any man to teach Paul, but instead chose to personally reveal himself to Paul. This means that, from the day of his conversion, Paul depended on revelation from God for direction in his life and ministry. Understand that all that Paul did and said was a product of revelation from Jesus; he was a man that lived by revelation. Revelation guided him on whom to associate with and whom not to associate with and it was by way of revelation that he connected with Titus. It is my personal opinion that the book of Galatians provides the best background Scripture regarding how Titus became a part of Paul's life:

Then after fourteen years I went up again to Jerusalem ***with Barnabas, taking Titus with me.*** *I went up* ***because of a revelation****...*
~Gal 2:1~

You will remember that Paul and Barnabas were chosen by God through the Word that was released by the prophets at Antioch (Acts 13:2-3). While they were worshiping and fasting, God instructed them to set apart Paul and Barnabas for the work of ministry. So Paul was with Barnabas because of an instruction from God. We later learn that Paul, also took Titus with him when they went to Jerusalem. It was from this time onwards that Titus started to follow Paul in the ministry as his spiritual son (he became a disciple and a follower of Paul). It is through this relationship that Titus grew to become the true and trusted son of Apostle Paul. Paul was so confident in his role as a spiritual father to an extent that he was ready to defend his role at any time.

I do not write these things to make you ashamed, but to admonish you as my ***beloved children.*** *For* ***though you have countless guides in Christ, you do not have many fathers.*** *For* ***I became your father in Christ Jesus through the gospel.***

~1Cor 4:14-15~

Paul wrote to his children in Corinth to admonish them. In his admonition, he addressed the issue of fatherhood. As children, the members of the church at Corinth seem to have been struggling with the issue of fatherhood and sonship. Paul did not mince his words, he made it clear to them that he was their father in Christ Jesus. He had become an example of Christ to them and he fathered and covered them in their walk with God. He was their source should they want to know of, or understand Christ. Since he referred to them as children, it is likely that they were still young in the Lord and perhaps they had not yet learned how to be led by the Holy Spirit. Paul came into their lives as a spiritual father to be a cover and a guider as they developed in the things of God. Through these verses, Paul emphasized his role as their father in order to clear any confusion about spiritual fatherhood.

He did not want his spiritual children to confuse their guides, or mentors with him as their spiritual father. He was their one and only spiritual father. In the same way that in the natural no single person is born of two fathers, so it is in the spiritual. In the same way that in the natural we do not chose or change our fathers, so it is in the spiritual. You spiritual father is your father by the sovereign choice of God, regardless of whatever flaws he may have, He is God's choice for you. Cover his nakedness and submit fully. It was through such a relationship that Titus grew to become the true and trusted son of Apostle Paul.

2

THE VALUE OF SONSHIP

And behold, a voice from heaven said, "This is my ***beloved Son****, with whom I am well pleased".*

~Mt 3:17~

When we read the account of the baptism of Jesus, we are often so drawn to the drama of the heavens opening and the voice of God speaking and we miss the revelation in what He said. This account is so powerful because it tells us deep truths about God's agenda on earth. Of all the references that God could have made concerning Jesus (Savior, King of Kings, Lion of the tribe of Judah etc.), He found the reference to a "son" as the most fitting. The first thing God wants to set clear is who Jesus was; He was the beloved Son of God. I am tempted to believe that "son" is the greatest title a person can have on earth.

If you think of all Jesus is and how all that is captured in one word "son", you will begin to value son-ship. Of all the relationships that God could have had with man, He chose that He wanted a relationship of sons because of all that God is, primarily, He is Abba Father. I pray that you are getting the revelation of what it means to be a son. Notice how when God refers to Jesus as His son, Jesus is already a fully grown man, yet He had only just became a Son. We are born children but we mature into sons!

The story of Abraham and his son, Isaac, is a remarkable story of radical obedience and faith in God. From that single account, there is a wealth of life principles that have timeless relevance. I want to draw from its richness in this chapter with the aim of helping you gain understanding of the value of sonship.

Abraham was called by God and was greatly blessed with flocks and herds, silver and gold, male servants and female servant (Gen 24:35). The number of all his servants is not given, but we are told that his trained servants alone were 318 (Gen 14:14). If the man needed 318 servants to ensure the efficient running of his household, we can confidently assume that he was a wealthy man. Yet despite all that he had amassed, and all those who served him, he was still not content, something was still missing, he did not have a son. One day, God spoke to Abraham in a vision promising him His personal protection and a great reward. Imagine, not only was he rich, but God was promising that He would ensure that he is protected and that he was guaranteed a great reward, that is enough to make most people ecstatic. However, Abraham was not excited. Instead, the Bible records the following:

> *But Abraham said, "Sovereign LORD,* ***what can you give me since I remain childless*** *and the one who will* ***inherit my estate is***

***Eliezer** of Damascus?"*
~Gen 15:2~

Abraham was not excited by the promises of God because he was childless, all the money and protection in the world, were nothing compared to the prospect of having a son, an heir. Abraham had many servants, but the fact is, they were not his children. A servant is very different from a child. The bond and love a father shares with his son cannot be compared to that of even the most trusted servant. Abraham had a trusted servant in his house called Eliezer, but he still ached to have a son that would receive all that was his as an inheritance. I do not want you to miss this, Eliezer was no ordinary servant to Abraham, he clearly had a special place in Abraham's heart, we see this when Abraham entrusts the task of finding a wife for his son (whom he loved so dearly) in the hands of Eliezer (Gen 24:3). Yet, Abraham was not happy with his servant getting his inheritance instead of his own son. This is because, the inheritance is not meant for servants but it is the exclusive portion of children. Whenever we find the portion of children going to servants, we know that this is abnormal or unusual. What belongs to the father is the portion of his children not his servants, servants get a salary and not an inheritance. The servant qualifies to receive from the father because he has worked; while the son qualifies because he was born in the family. The servant is entitled to his pay by contract; the son is entitled to an inheritance by birthright. This is why even if there are grown-up and mature servants in the house and a young child who is entitled to the inheritance, the inheritance will be put aside until the child has matured enough to steward his inheritance rather than to give the inheritance to the servant (Gal 4:1). The child is always the first preference for the inheritance. Remember, not only was Abraham wealthy; the promises of

God upon his life were also great, too great to go into the hands of a servant.

The secret things belong to the
LORD our God, but the ***things***
that are revealed belong to us
and to our children forever...
~Deut 29:29~

The above Scripture is a "master key" to understanding spiritual inheritance. In essence, God is saying, the secret things (the realms of revelation and power that you do not know) belong to Him, but the secret things of God that fathers travail in the spirit to access, become an inheritance for their children forever. If

I, as a father; have been graced by God to know great realms of the power and the glory of God, if I have been able to access great level of understanding and revelation of the Word of God, that becomes a spiritual inheritance for my spiritual children. They do not have to work to learn and access those things from scratch, but they receive it as an inheritance from me as their father. The inheritance becomes an advantage, they do not need to start where I did, instead, they start where I left off.

I am a man that God has given much revelation and great access into the realms of the prophetic, healing and deliverance. All that I have learnt and tapped into is now an inheritance for my sons! This is why Paul took time to train his sons, because they would one day have to be stewards of all that he would leave behind as an inheritance. The father becomes immortal through his sons, they carry his vision long after his death and all that he has worked for. Sons are a guarantee that the legacy of the father will continue long after his death, wherever the son is, the father's name will be promoted. Titus was this guarantee to Paul; that his spiritual inheritance was in the right hands. Remember that a son is like the father, which is why Jesus could boldly say that when you had seen Him, you had seen the Father. I don't care how faithful and obedient a servant may be, he is always like his father and not like his master. If he receives an inheritance from his master, he will lay it up for his own sons. A servant can never make the name of the father great, only a son can. A family name is what ensures continuity. The "Bushiri" name has continued long after the first "Bushiri" because there has been generations of sons like myself that have kept that lineage going till today. Without a son, the name of Abraham and all that it stood for faced extinction and this made the concern of Abraham very valid. It was only through a son that he was guaranteed to have his name being great among the nations (Gen 12 &15).

Through the years we have lost understanding of the value of a great name. In biblical times, a name was extremely prophetic; it affected destinies hence it had to be protected. That is why it is only those who are led by the Spirit that qualify to be called sons of God. This is because if they are led by the Spirit, they will be ensuring the continuity of the character of God. This is very important because if they are led by any other spirit, they will not be reproducing the character of God but of that which is leading them and this makes the name of God vulnerable to being tainted. Like Abraham, I, as a prophet of God, and a father of many spiritual children, I am not content to have church members who are just servants; instead, I am looking for those children who will take a stand and become sons. I can entrust all that God has given me into the hands of sons not servants. I believe that this is the cry of every man of God; we do not want all that we have tarried for in the spirit to die when we die, but we want sons who will go forth with the inheritance and do greater works than we were able to do.

3

THE COMPETENT SON

Titus was not just a son to Paul, but was also a competent son. In the previous chapter, I pointed out that Paul chose Titus as his son by way of revelation. It was the revelation that Paul had about Titus, that led him to love him so much. This is very important to note because not every man of God is your father and not every church member is a son. As God began to increasingly use me on an international platform, many men of God started searching for me, asking to be my spiritual sons. I have rejected many of them because I discerned by revelation that they were not meant to be my sons. Whenever God gives me a new son he often tells me that, "I am giving you so and so as a son and as a gift to you". I can assure you now, that when God gives you a true son, that son becomes a special gift from God in your life. It may not sit well with religious people but the truth is that there are certain people that God specifically created to serve as a gift to a man of God. Their unique purpose on earth is to be a gift and a blessing to the man of God.

And behold, I have taken ***your brothers the Levites;*** *from among the people of Israel. They are a* ***gift to you****, given to the LORD, to do the* ***service of the tent of meeting****.*
~Num 18:6~

Aaron's brothers, the Levites; were given to Aaron by God for the sole purpose of being a gift to Aaron. Believe it or not, God gives people away as gifts! Remember that the Levites were a peculiar people because God chose them specifically to minister to Him in the tent of meeting; however, they did this as a gift to Aaron. Note that even though they ministered unto God, they were not a *gift to God*, but a *gift to Aaron*! God saw it fit to give Aaron these men as gifts to fulfill the work of the priesthood. Meaning that, without these "gifts", being a High Priest would have been burdensome to Aaron. Similarly, there are people with great anointing and skills whom God has prepared, not for their own ministries but to be a gift to the man of God. To employ their gifts to serve the man of God as he serves God. Paul knew that for him to do the work that God had given him as a priest and apostle, he needed gifts like Titus. God had also equipped Titus with skills and abilities (competencies) for this work as well.

To best describe the competency of Titus, I would like to draw Timothy into the picture. It would be a grave injustice to speak about sonship, particularly as far as Paul is concerned without mentioning Timothy. Like Titus, Timothy was also a spiritual son to Paul. With the number of churches that Paul was overseeing, I am certain he had many sons who were assisting him in ministry. Of all his sons, Paul makes explicit mention of Titus and Timothy the most, meaning that there was something peculiar about the two. As we read the Bible, we learn that the two shared similarities; aside from the fact that they were both the sons of Paul, they both seem to have joined the ministry very young. In the letters that Paul wrote to both of them, he emphasized that they should not allow anyone to despise them and he said this in reference to their age (Tit 2:15; 1Tim 4:12). It is because of their age that Paul requested them to live an exemplary life (Tit 2:7; 1Tim 4:12). Although Paul never referred to them by any ministerial title beside the fact that they were his sons, they were involved in the apostolic work within the ministry of Paul. He would send them to do some work in different cities where he had branches.

Yet another commonality between Titus and Timothy is that both their books (letters) that Paul wrote to them, were pastoral in nature. They are so named, because they primarily concerned themselves with ministerial issues such as raising leaders in the church. Despite these similarities there is a noticeable difference between the tones of the two letters. There are things that Paul said to Titus in his letter that were never said to Timothy and vice-versa. One of the distinct differences that I would like to pull your attention to, is the sternness and soundness in doctrine of Titus as compared to Timothy. Although Timothy knew the ways of Paul and was sent by Paul to teach at various branches, Paul still instructed him to immerse himself more in the Word, something we never hear Paul say to Titus (1Cor 4:17; 2Tim 2:15). Although they both had to oversee certain churches in Corinth, Titus seemed to have been often assigned to the more difficult churches. One of the difficult churches that Paul sent Titus to, was to the believers in Crete. In his letter to Titus, Paul wrote:

*One of the Cretans, a prophet of their own, said, "**Cretans are always liars, evil beasts, lazy gluttons**". **This testimony is true.** Therefore **rebuke them sharply,** that they may be **sound in the faith**.*

~Tit 1:12~

Lazy, liars and evil gluttons, these are the kinds of people that Titus was commissioned to. I believe that Paul sent Titus not Timothy to this group of people knowing that Titus had in him the ability to handle the situation in Crete. Paul even went on to ask Titus to sharply rebuke the Cretans. I believe that Paul could have only gave such an instruction to Titus because he knew he had the boldness and sternness to successfully execute the task at hand. Have you ever wondered why in the Parable of the talents, the different servants are entrusted with different amounts? I have discovered that it is because God already knew what each servant had the ability to faithfully steward. He knew that the first servant could be trusted with five talents without the talents overwhelming or corrupting him. The same for the second servant and the third servant, they were trusted with two talents and one talent, respectively. It would have been unfair for God to give them more than they had the ability to manage. The same principle is at work here, Paul knew what his sons had ability to handle and portioned their assignments according to their abilities. Both were equally his sons, Paul even referred to them as brothers, but of Titus he said, "My partner" (2Cor 8:23). This means, Titus matured to a level that Paul could refer to him as his partner. He saw him as having the same spirit as him. Paul writes to the Corinthians:

Did I take advantage of you through any of those whom I sent to you? ***I urged Titus to go****, and*

sent the brother with him. Did Titus take advantage of you? Did ***we not act in the same spirit? Did we not take the same steps?***
~2Cor 12:17-18~

Paul is essentially saying that he and Titus were one in what they did. The two were in-sync to such an extent that not only was Titus a son who knew the acts of his father, but he also operated in the same spirit as him, he knew his ways. It is one thing to know the acts of a man but it's another thing to know his ways. This is what separated Moses from the Israelites who only knew what God did but never why He did it (Ps

103:7). When you know the ways of a man, you know what is in his heart and spirit not just the external manifestation thereof. Titus enjoyed fellowship with Paul so much so, that Paul had to urge him to go to Corinth. I relate with this so well because I have had sons who are so eager to go off to head their own branches because they do not want to submit. There is absolutely nothing wrong with submitting to another man while having your own ministry but I can tell you now, the level of fellowship that the sons who live in the house enjoy is different than the one that those who live out of the house enjoy. By the same token the degree of submission required from those in the house is greater than those outside the house. You know how it is when you are in you fathers' house, it is his house and his rules. When you move out of the house you keep some of his rules and you discard others. It is amusing yet sad to watch what some sons do. Some would rather have a dead church with 15 members and be a "father" in that church than to submit as a son under a man with a great ministry, where the power and presence of God is.

Paul further records the following about Titus:

But thanks be to God, ***who put into the heart of Titus the same earnest care I have for you.***

~2Cor 8:16~

Over and above having the same spirit as Paul, Titus had in his heart, the same earnest care that Paul had. Few things in ministry life surpass the joy of having sons who care about what you care about, whose food is to do the will of their father. Titus cared for the Corinthians with the same intensity that Paul cared for them. His heart was so intricately woven with the heart of his father that he knew what concerned him. The body of Christ is in desperate need of such manner of sons. We have many sons in the house but far too few sons like Titus. Where are the Titus's?

4

THE TRUE SON

In the second chapter I pointed out that God could have referred to Jesus using any one of His more majestic and powerful titles such as, *Saviour, King of Kings, Lion of the tribe of Judah* and so forth, yet instead, He opted for the title of a son. Paul did the same in the letter that he wrote to Titus, in his first reference to Titus, he said:

*To **Titus my true son** in our common faith...*
~Tit 1:4~

Titus was not just a son to Paul, but a true son, a son with whom he shared common faith. The word, "common", speaks of something being the same as, meaning that Titus had the same type, quality and quantity of faith as that of Paul. Common faith does not only refer to the same belief, instead, it also implies that Titus had the same level of faith as that of Paul. Meaning, what Paul had the ability to believe God for; Titus could also believe God for the same. They were that connected in faith. Again, for Paul to refer to Titus as a true son, it means that there are also false sons. Through ministry, I have learned that there are different kinds of sons, namely:

sons in *need*

sons *indeed*

sons in *deeds*.

Sons in *need* are people who become sons in response to a need they have in their lives which they believe that by having you as their spiritual father, their needs will be met. Such sons are never there for your ministry or vision, instead, they come to grab what they can for their own ministries and vision. Sons in *need* do not care much for what you want or need; instead, the focus is always on what they can leech from you. You can list all your needs to them, but they will never bring you a solution or offer to help. Instead, they will add their needs to your to-do list. Paul had a son like this whose name was Demas. It is recorded of him:

For Demas in love with this present world, has deserted me and gone to Thessalonica.

~2Tim 4:10~

Demas was a spiritual son of Paul, but due to his love for the present world, he deserted Paul (Col 4:14; Philm 24). Such behavior is typical of sons in *need*, they either get what they want from you and leave or they leave because you are not giving them what they want. When a son in *need* sees that his needs are not met in the house, he looks for satisfaction outside and when he finds it, he leaves. Demas was such a kind of a son; the world gave him more satisfaction than being a son to Paul hence he deserted him.

The second category of sons is that of sons *indeed*. These are sons whom, if you are not careful to discern them beyond face value, they can easily deceive you. They are big on talking and small on doing. They say all the right things, but do all the wrong things. The Cretans fell under this category of sons. Paul described them in this way:

They ***profess to know God****, but*
they ***deny him by their works****.*
They are ***detestable, disobedient,***
unfit for any good work*.*
~Tit 1:16~

Paul described them as detestable, disobedient and unfit of any good work. They were detestable because they were against the vision of their spiritual father, disobedient because they never did what they promised, and were unfit for any good work because they lacked the skills to do what they claim they would do. They are like one of the sons in the parable of the two sons. When the father requested the sons to go to the vineyard, one of the sons refused but later changed his mind and went, while the other one agreed but never did what he promised to do (see Mt 21:28-32). The brother who agreed but never did what he promised to do, is typical of a son *indeed,* they are full of words but empty on works. That is why Paul referred to them as empty talkers and unfit for good works.

The last category of sons is that of sons in *deeds*. These are sons who do good works. Unlike the sons *indeed*, sons in deeds have deeds that support what they confess. In his letter to Titus, Paul stated:

> *And let our people learn to devote themselves to* ***good works****, so as to help cases of urgent need, and not be unfruitful.*
>
> ~Tit 3:14~

Paul instructed Titus to teach people to devote themselves to good works. Titus had to have had good works in his own account for him to teach others about good works. He was not just a son, but a true son who was a son in *deeds*. Not only did he speak, but he did what he confessed or promised to do. He is a great example of a true son and Paul loved him dearly for this. In his closing instruction to Titus, he said:

When I send Artemas or Tychicus to you, ***do your best to come to me at Nicopolis, for I have decided to spend the winter there****.*

~Tit 3:12~

Winter is an uncomfortable time; the days are dark, cold and lonely in winter. The Bible tells us that the tribulation of the end times will be worse if it takes place in winter (Mt 24:20). However, despite the discomfort of winter, Paul asked Titus to come to Nicopolis where he had decided to spend the winter. A request only made to Titus and Timothy (see also, 2 Tim 4:21). Paul seems to be calling Titus to be with him as his comfort during the winter season. Don't miss the revelation here, winter can also speak of a gloomy and cold season in your life. So what Paul is essentially saying is, in the gloom of the winter season, the presence of his son Titus will make the winter more bearable. There are sons whose presence during the winter season of persecutions and trials, become a fountain of comfort and strength. It is undeniable that Paul and Titus had an unusual bond and the Scriptures testify to this fact. The verse below serves as another example, Paul reveals something that one would never think of him or any man of God doing. Read the words of Paul below:

When I came to Troas to preach the gospel of Christ, even though a door was opened for me in the Lord, my spirit was not at rest because I did not find my brother

Titus there. So I took leave *of them and went on to Macedonia.*
~2Cor 2:12-13~

Paul was a man that was led by the Holy Spirit in all his ministry endeavors (Acts 16:6; 1Cor 16:9). He would only go where the Holy Spirit was leading him to. In the above verse we are told that he went to Troas because God had opened a door for him. What is intriguing about this is that, when he did not find Titus at Troas, he stopped the crusade and left the place! Just imagine that, an apostle of Paul's stature, leaving a crusade just because of the absence of his spiritual son, Titus. Imagine all the sick who were waiting to be healed, the oppressed who were eagerly waiting to be delivered through the ministration of Paul. Yet Paul left all of them hanging because his precious son was not there. What a connection! Paul mentions that his spirit was not at rest because of the absence of Titus. The same spirit that Paul mentioned was connected to Titus was not at rest because the one whom he connected to in spirit was not there. Because of this, Paul decided to discontinue the crusade even though God had opened a door for him to be there. Let that sink in. Paul chose to be passed by an opportunity that God had made available for him, just because he could not bear the absence of his spiritual son. Titus was not just a son, but he was a true son that was knit to the heart of his father. The Bible also records the following about Titus:

For even when we came into Macedonia, ***our bodies had no rest****, but we were afflicted at every turn- fighting without and fear within.* ***But God, who comforts the downcast, comforted us by the coming of Titus...***

~2Cor 7:5-6~

Paul and his team had a difficult time at Macedonia, they faced affliction, however; they were comforted and re-energized by the coming of Titus. Through this book I hope to incite you, to not only carry the title of a competent son; but to also become a deep well of joy to your spiritual father.

5

CHARACTERISTICS OF TITUS

I will be doing injustice if I end this book without referring to certain key characteristics of Titus that distinguished him from all of the sons of Apostle Paul. I draw these characteristics from the letter that Paul wrote to Titus.

Characteristic #1: Obedience To the

Voice of His Spiritual Father

> ***The reason I left you in Crete*** *was that you might put in order what was left unfinished and appoint elders in every town, as I directed you.*
>
> ~Tit 1:5~

Paul wrote this letter to Titus who was already at Crete. In the letter he was explaining to him the reason why he left him there! This means, when Paul left Titus in Crete, he possibly never gave him a reason why he was leaving him there; however, Titus obeyed the voice of his father and remained behind. Out of obedience, Titus remained in Crete with "*liars, evil beasts, lazy gluttons*" without even knowing the reason why he was there. It was only later, through the letter that he came to understand why he was left behind in Crete. This kind of radical obedience can only be found in true sons. At times there are things that I do for no other reason aside from the fact that my spiritual father, the voice of God in my life has said so. I do what my spiritual father commands, whether or not I understand is irrelevant, I just do because through him I believe that God has said I should do that thing. Sons who insist on understanding before they obey can quench the flow of the Spirit at work in me. I find it easy to father and work with sons who are like Titus, who just obey my voice as their father without questioning; such obedience gives me the confidence as the father that I am trusted by my sons. I have a caution here: I only follow my father and his instructions because he follows Christ. Please do not just follow anyone because they have the title of a 'prophet' or a 'pastor', follow only if they follow Christ!

Characteristic #2: A Leader Who Led an Exemplary Life

The reason I left you in Crete was

*that **you might put in order what was left unfinished and appoint elders** in every town, as I directed you.*
~Tit 1:5~

Paul left Titus at Crete so that he could put the churches in order and appoint elders. Anyone who has been in church leadership knows that it is very difficult to control church leaders, especially if you are not their spiritual father. Titus was a son to Paul, a brother to the Cretans, yet he was given this task. Paul assigned this massive assignment to Titus because he was confident in his ability to lead his fellow brothers and sisters in the

Lord correctly. For Paul to trust that the Cretans would listen to Titus, it means Titus must have possessed qualities which demonstrated that he had in him all that was necessary to successfully lead the believers in Crete.

Characteristic #3: A Good Teacher of Sound Doctrine

*You, however, must **teach what is appropriate to sound doctrine**.*

~Tit 2:1~

One of the assignments that Paul gave to Titus was to teach sound doctrine. There were people in Crete who were teaching things which were not doctrinally sound, and Paul commissioned Titus to correct this error (Tit 1:11). For Titus to do this, he had to have been well grounded in the doctrines that Paul taught in order to teach them to others. Some sons have their own doctrines that are contrary to that of their spiritual father yet they want to teach them to the people that God has entrusted to the care of their father. If you do not agree with the teachings of your father, talk to God about it and let Him guide you but do not teach your own teachings in your father's house! That flock is under his care and he must account for those souls before God not you. Besides, a father raises his sons to be like him and as a son, do not try to raise your brothers to be like you. Remember, what makes siblings to look alike is because of the genes that they get from their parents not each other. There can only be one vision bearer and one father in the house and everyone else is a product of that vision and submits to it, therefore, you need to know your place in that equation!

Characteristic #4: Subject to Rulers and Authorities

*Remind the people to be **subject to rulers and authorities**...*

~Tit 3:1~

Paul requested of Titus that he remind people to be subject to rulers and authorities. He could confidently ask this of Titus because Titus himself was subject to him as a ruler and authority in his life. This is one of the biggest challenges in churches, lack of submission to those who have been put in authority. I am still amazed by some of my children who claim to be submissive to me but do not submit under those whom I put over them. As a spiritual father, I do not measure the submission of a son by how they submit to me only; instead, I also measure their submission by how they submit to those whom I have put over them. That is a sure sign of a true son.

There are so many more things I wish to teach you on this subject but you are not yet ready to hear them. I pray that what I have taught here will challenge you to rise up into maturity and claim your place in the life of the father that God has given you as a true, faithful, competent and obedient son of whom your father can be well pleased!

Shalom!!!

ABOUT THE AUTHOR

Prophet Shepherd Bushiri is the president and founder of Shepherd Bushiri Ministries International and Enlightened Christian Gathering (EGG) Church. ECG has its headquarters in Pretoria, South Africa and has branches across the African continent. Prophet Shepherd Bushiri is used mightily by God in the prophetic, healing and deliverance and has a massive following on his TV Channel, Prophetic Channel. His ministry is also known as 'the ministry of the book of Acts' because of the undeniable signs and wonders which happen in the name of Jesus. His prophecies are marked by great accuracy and precision. Through his mysterious birth, he came into this world with one mandate from God, "go and prove that I (God) exist and I am still speaking even today" and he is fulfilling his mandate with excellence.

BOOKS BY THE AUTHOR

- The Pursuit of Titus: Unveiling True Sonship
- The Prophetic Calling
- Tongues: Revelations of the Heavenly language
- Breaking Bloodline Curses
- Destroying Leviathan Spirits
- Breaking Evil foundations
- The School of Prophets and The Prophetic Ministry
- The Process of Receiving the Anointing
- The Spiritual Battlefield

46252616R00049

Printed in Poland
by Amazon Fulfillment
Poland Sp. z o.o., Wrocław